RACE CAR LEGENDS

CHELSEA HOUSE PUBLISHERS

RACE CAR LEGENDS

THE MAKING OF A RACE CAR

Richard Huff

CHELSEA HOUSE PUBLISHERS
Philadelphia

Frontis: Mark Martin in the Valvoline Taurus Ford running test laps to tune the new car early in the 1998 season.

Produced by Type Shoppe II Productions, Ltd.
Chestertown, Maryland

Picture research by Joseph W. Wagner

CHELSEA HOUSE PUBLISHERS

Editor in Chief: Stephen Reginald
Managing Editor: James Gallagher
Production Manager: Pamela Loos
Art Director: Sara Davis
Photo Editor: Judy L. Hasday
Senior Production Editor: Lisa Chippendale
Publishing Coordinator: James McAvoy
Cover Illustration: Keith Trego

Cover Photos: front cover: CIA Stock; back cover: CIA Stock/Ernest Masche

3 5 7 9 8 6 4 2

The Chelsea House Publishers World Wide Web site address is
http://www.chelseahouse.com

Library of Congress Cataloging-in-Publication Data
Huff, Richard M.
     The making of a race car / Richard Huff.
          p.   cm. — (Race car legends)
     Includes bibliographical references and index.
     Summary: Describes the developments in the design and construction of race cars sanctioned by NASCAR from their early days during Prohibition to the current custom-built cars.
     ISBN 0-7910-5020-3 (alk. paper)
     1. Automobiles, Racing—Juvenile literature. 2. Stock car racing—United States—Juvenile literature. 3. NASCAR (Association)—Juvenile literature. [1. Automobiles, Racing—Design and construction.] I. Title. II. Series.
TL236.H84 1998
629.228—dc21

                                                           98-19230
                                                               CIP
                                                               AC

CONTENTS

HOW IT ALL GOT STARTED

Although they are called stock cars, the label couldn't be further from the truth for the vehicles used for racing in the National Association for Stock Car Auto Racing's (NASCAR) top level. The brightly painted Fords, Chevrolets, and Pontiacs driven by men such as Mark Martin, Dale Earnhardt, and Kyle Petty aren't simply stripped down and souped up versions of the street-legal models sold by the dealer around the corner.

They look the same as the street models, but the cars driven on NASCAR's premiere series circuit are highly efficient, specially built race cars. They are built for speed, not comfort. There are no cup holders, no glove compartments, no rear-window defrosters, and no passenger seats.

There is room for only one: the driver. Anybody else would simply weigh the car down, and in racing, every ounce counts. In

A group of cars on the track at the start of a NASCAR race shows the individual designs utilized to distinguish sponsors and teams.

NASCAR racing, it is driver and machine against the rest of the field, and if all goes well, the smartest driver with the fastest car wins.

Today's cars are handcrafted from the ground up by trained mechanics who use 1990s technology based on designs that evolved in the 1960s. The roots of the sport, however, date back much earlier than that.

Stock car racing is a decidedly American phenomenon that started in the 1930s. Back then, drinking alcoholic beverages was illegal. However, many independent businessmen continued to make alcoholic drinks and hired drivers to ship the product throughout the

Twenty-five years at Daytona— Bill France Sr. looks out at his track, the Daytona International Speedway, which he built in 1969.

South. The drivers modified their cars to outrun the police when they were on their delivery runs. Routinely drivers took out all of the seats to make room for the alcohol and to lower the overall weight. They would also tweak the motor to gain as much horsepower (hp) as possible.

And when drivers weren't trying to outrun the police, they turned to racing against each other. Often, arguments over who was fastest were settled on a makeshift track set up in an empty cornfield. Those races attracted locals who cheered on the drivers. When some people, looking to make money, figured out they could stage formal races and charge fans to watch, organized stock car racing was born.

In most cases the events went smoothly, although there were some unscrupulous race organizers who ran off with the prize money before the race was over.

Then along came William Henry Getty "Bill" France. France was a mechanic from Washington, D.C., who in 1934 decided to move to Daytona Beach, Florida. He became friends with people who were racing in Daytona at the time and drove in the first stock car race held on the beach at Daytona in 1936. He finished fifth.

France promoted the races in Daytona and soon promoted races at tracks throughout the South. At the same time, crooked promoters were giving the sport a bad name. France longed for an organization that could control the sport.

In December 1947, France called a group of his friends together and at a series of meetings at the Streamline Hotel in Daytona Beach created the plan for NASCAR. It was to be a sanctioning body which would preside over a series of races for modern cars. NASCAR was incorporated in February 1948 and held its first race on February 15, 1948.

The rules were simple: the cars had to be the same as those on the showroom floor. If the car had a bench seat in the front, it had to have it on the race track. Drivers raced on grooved street tires in cars with virtually no safety equipment. France and NASCAR believed people wanted to see new cars race instead of junkyard bombs.

In the early days of the sport, drivers raced cars with working doors, windows, and headlights. Most drove their cars to the track, applied numbers to the sides with duct tape, and then, provided they didn't wreck the cars, drove them back home. Even in the 1960s, when cars reached speeds of up to 150 mph, drivers had cars with back seats and original floor carpeting. In fact, legendary driver Herb Thomas said he used his car radio when he raced!

Over time the cars evolved and changed as street cars became more sophisticated. Improvements to the cars usually came after on-track incidents which opened the eyes of promoters and racers to the need for more sophisticated modifications. In fact, virtually all of the safety devices in place today came as a result of crashes that occurred in the early years of the sport. For example, roll bars, now an integral part of the safety structure of any stock car, started out as crude frames built with boards or plumber's pipe. Drivers used ropes, and later airplane pilots' belts, to harness themselves in cars when seatbelts were

not part of the standard equipment.

The fuel cell, a rubberized container that protects racing gasoline in crashes and prevents fires, was developed in the 1960s after some disastrous accidents.

NASCAR vehicles underwent their greatest changes in the 1960s when the auto manufacturers heavily backed the sport. Car makers

Mario Andretti (#13) in a 1964 Ford is trying to pass Bobby Allison (#24), driving a 1966 Ford, in the 100-mile qualifying race for the Daytona 500. Allison had to retire from the race when his car began to smoke.

lived under the rule, "Win on Sunday, Sell on Monday," and it was important for their cars to take the checkered flag most often. Auto manufacturers thought if a Ford won a stock car race, the fans would want one, too, and they invested in making sure their cars won.

NASCAR originally mandated that automakers produce a minimum of 500 models of the cars raced for sale to the public. Some car makers took that literally, and created special models for the race track but produced the bare minimum for car dealers. Eventually NASCAR upped the minimums by forcing the manufacturers to actually race the models available to the general public.

Today, the only similarities stock cars have to their street-legal siblings is basic body style. Under NASCAR rules, the car bodies, whether Monte Carlo or Grand Prix, must fit a series of templates modeled after the production version.

Of the sheet-metal skin, only the roof, trunk lid, and hood are the same as the ones that come off the production line. The rest of the body is handmade.

While auto manufacturers have been relying on computers to control many of the functions on their street cars, such as the ignition and fuel injection, drivers in other racing series use them to determine gas mileage, to adjust engine performance, and to relay information back to their crews. NASCAR, however, prohibits any such on-board devices and wants control of the car to remain with the driver. Teams are permitted to use computers in practice but not during the race itself.

Although technology has advanced in the

making of street cars, it has actually stood still in the world of stock car racing, mostly for the benefit of the sport. Because computers cost money and the teams with the most money would likely have an unfair advantage, NASCAR prefers to keep their competitions as evenly matched and as fair as possible.

2

RACE CAR OR FAMILY CAR?

If you stripped away the rainbow-colored graphics, removed the "No. 24" from the roof and doors, and took off the Goodyear Eagle racing slicks, the Chevrolet Monte Carlo driven by two-time Winston Cup champion Jeff Gordon would, in many ways, resemble the same Monte Carlo you can buy at your local car dealership.

It is not an exact duplicate but definitely bears a close resemblance. The same is true of the Ford Taurus and the Pontiac Grand Prix. But that is where the similarities end, because even if a race car looks like a Monte Carlo or a Grand Prix or flies like a Taurus, it is a very different creature under the hood.

In order to make better race cars, NASCAR allows car manufacturers to change the body style of racers ever so slightly to improve the way the car moves through the air on the

Jeff Gordon stops for fuel on lap 391 of a race at Dover Downs International Raceway. Gordon led most of the race until this pit stop but eventually lost to Dale Jarrett.

track and to make the various car brands reasonably similar in performance. For example, the width of a Monte Carlo used for racing is slightly larger than that of a production model.

Although it is called stock car racing, there isn't much stock on today's racers. These cars are highly tuned vehicles built specifically for racing.

It wasn't always that way. When Bill France and his group of race track promoters from around the country got together in that Daytona Beach hotel and formed NASCAR, one of the new organization's basic tenants was that drivers use showroom model cars.

France argued that fans didn't want to watch jalopies race. Instead, they wanted to see reasonably new cars battling for the checkered flag. NASCAR launched its strictly stock series in February 1948. It was just that, too. With few exceptions, drivers were not allowed to modify their cars. In fact, any driver caught doing something to his car that wasn't available to the average customer buying the same car from a local dealer was penalized.

In 1949, Glenn Dunnaway won the first race in the strictly stock division. After the race, inspectors found a wedge jammed into his car's rear springs. Away from the track, Dunnaway spent time delivering illegally made alcohol in the South. Back then, jamming a wedge into the springs was a common practice that made the car ride higher when loaded with bottles of moonshine. But Dunnaway never removed the wedge and after winning was stripped of his victory by NASCAR.

Eventually NASCAR loosened its rules as technology changed. When special racing tires were developed, NASCAR allowed drivers to remove their street tires, and as safety became more of a factor, NASCAR allowed teams to install roll-bar systems to protect drivers in the event of a crash. Because metal gas tanks exploded during crashes, NASCAR allowed teams to use rubber fuel cells.

The team owners, drivers, and mechanics usually supported these changes. If, for example, they noticed that a roof caved in when a car rolled over, the teams were usually the first to try to figure out a solution.

By the mid 1960s, the cars were becoming less stock and more like the sleek racers of today. Instead of driving cars to the track,

Joe Gibbs (right), owner of the McDonald's car, and mechanic Larry Frazier (left) look over the remains of their car at the Winston Select Finals in Pomona, California. The car disintegrated after an engine explosion during qualifying. The driver was not injured because of safety features installed in the car during its construction.

many teams used trailers and haulers. Yet the basic premise of the sport, that versions of the cars used on the track must be available to consumers, remains intact.

But don't expect the car in the local Ford dealership to look anything like the ones driven by Rusty Wallace or Dale Jarrett. Race cars have no doors or door handles. Instead, drivers ease their bodies through the 16-inch-high opening where the window belongs. There are no passenger seats. Race cars only have room for the driver. And there is no such thing as a tilt wheel on a race car. Steering wheels are built to fit the specifications of the driver of the car.

Dale Jarrett climbs into his Kellogg's-sponsored Ford Taurus through the window.

Developing a street model for the race track takes years of work at the auto manufacturer's factory. In 1998, Ford decided that its widely popular Taurus model of family sedans would be its race car in the future. The Taurus replaced the Thunderbird, which, although popular at one time, was not selling well and was canceled by the manufacturer.

Take a walk around your local Ford dealer's lot and look for a Taurus with no doors. You won't find one. You won't find one with two doors, either. The street model Taurus is a four-door-only vehicle. However, to make it race worthy, NASCAR allowed Ford to tinker with the body style and doors.

And Chevrolet doesn't make a Monte Carlo with rear-wheel drive. In fact, all of the cars racing in NASCAR events in the 1990s are available to consumers as front-wheel drive models only, another concession but also a throwback to the sport's early days when rear-wheel drive was the norm.

With each new model, NASCAR issues teams a set of templates, or patterns, from which to build their cars. The templates are a combination of patterns that come directly from the showroom models and the automakers. "There are 18 templates approved and issued [in 1998] that apply to the Taurus," said Preston Miller, Ford's NASCAR technical manager. "Of those 18 templates, nine fit the production [street model] car. Of the nine we don't fit, the long template hasn't fit any production car competing in NASCAR since back in the 1980s, because the back of the hood and the cowl were raised for the engine package. Then there are six templates,

A Chevrolet engine prior to being installed into a NASCAR competition vehicle.

like the door template, that [don't] fit any of the production cars, because [of] the width of the tail and the tail area."

Prior to the start of the 1998 season, Pontiac and Chevrolet drivers complained that the new Taurus as adapted for racing by Ford was so far away from the original design that it didn't resemble the family sedan. Miller answered the complaint by saying that there really isn't such a thing as a stock car any more, citing the lack of doors, windows, and the inclusion of roll bars in each of the models, especially the Chevrolets. "If that's a stock car, then I haven't seen one for sale in a dealership in a long time," Miller said. "And you're not going to see one, either, not a Taurus, not a Monte Carlo and not a Grand Prix. Even [NASCAR president] Bill France says that we haven't raced a stock car in many years."

Underneath the sheet metal, the three makes of cars that run on the Winston Cup and Busch Grand National series are very similar. In fact, some parts on the three makes are exactly the same.

They each start off with a hand-built chassis made with rectangular steel tubing and a tubular roll cage. The highest point in the roof line is no more than 51 inches. The cars cannot weight more than 3,600 pounds, including the driver. Each vehicle must have a wheelbase of 110 inches, and all are equipped with a manual, four-speed transmission. They all use the same 9.5" x 15" steel wheels, each has a four-barrel Holley 750-830 carburetor bolted onto a 358-cubic-inch (c.i.) V-8 engine, all are capable of producing more than 700 hp, and all are fitted with four-wheel disc brakes.

The main difference among the three makes of race cars is in the engine. Chevrolets use Chevrolet motors, Fords use Ford motors, and Pontiacs use General Motors engines. For example, the three street-legal cars each carry six-cylinder, 231 c.i. engines capable of producing up to 240 hp, or about one third of what the Winston Cup engines turn out. The street cars use five quarts of oil, again, one third of what the Winston Cup cars carry. And Winston Cup cars use traditional carburetors, whereas their street sisters use electronically controlled fuel injection.

FROM THE
GROUND UP

Beneath the sheet metal bodies and the motors, all stock cars rest on a chassis.

The chassis, or frame, is the equivalent of a human skeleton. The chassis holds the parts of the car together in a sturdy fashion, much the way a skeleton provides a form for the flesh, muscles, and organs of the human body. And like a skeleton, if one part of the chassis fails, it can cause the rest of the machine to perform improperly.

Chassis have been part of cars since the first ones were put together in the late 1800s. From the start, and through the 1970s, all cars were built on hardened steel frames, which in some ways resembled a ladder with two long arms running the length of the car and shorter bars crossing between them to hold up the components.

Under NASCAR's early rules, the frame used by car manufacturers to build their cars had

The rear view of a complete chassis, showing the shock absorbers, oversize oil tank, seat belts, side steel tubing, and roll cage protection.

to be incorporated into the racing models. This, along with everything else on today's racers, evolved with the times, and eventually NASCAR allowed teams to add extra steel to the chassis to beef up the suspension. Later, as the need for a roll cage became apparent, the rules changed again to make it an integral part of the chassis.

Although NASCAR was able to hold onto its stock roots into the 1960s, the sport changed dramatically in the 1970s. Teams began to build their own tubular steel chassis. The reasons were simple: first, it made more sense to create their own chassis, which allowed them to position key suspension parts; and second, Detroit automakers were slowly moving away from traditional car frame formats to ones in which the chassis and body were inseparable. As a result, it was difficult for teams to modify the new street-legal models for racing. Although it took several more years for the full changeover to occur, it was clear in the 1970s that the sport was headed in a direction where the outward appearance of the car—the bodies—would remain stock but the internal workings would be specifically designed for racing.

In fact, the rudimentary design of today's handcrafted chassis is similar to the one introduced in the 1970s. Teams have modified the concept as technology has allowed and for safety reasons, but the basic concept remains the same.

Why is the chassis so important? Think about a skeleton. If a person breaks a leg, the way he or she walks is likely to be affected. It is the same with a chassis. If all parts of the chassis—the frame rails, the crossmembers, the suspension mounting points—are not perfectly aligned, the car will not handle properly on the track.

Some teams, such as Roush Racing and Hendrick Motorsports, build their own chassis, using their own designs and specifications, which are based on NASCAR's rule book. Building a chassis in their shop allows them to know exactly what materials are being used, tinker with the positioning of certain mounting brackets for the body and suspension parts, and attempt to duplicate a chassis that the driver likes. It also lets the team control the production cycle. With all forms of NASCAR racing booming, the demand for the basic chassis has increased, creating a backlog in many of the major chassis manufacturers.

A Robert Yates racing team member works on the chassis of a Ford Taurus in anticipation of the change from the Thunderbird body to the Ford Taurus for the 1998 NASCAR racing season.

The downside to chassis built by the race team is the cost. Overall costs increase because the team has to maintain people on its payroll to build the chassis and have an area of the shop allotted only to working with the steel to build the frames. Buying premade chassis is less expensive because a team owner does not have to hire specialized crew members or buy the necessary equipment.

NASCAR teams which do not build their own chassis tend to buy them from one of three manufacturers: Laughlin Race Products, Hutcherson-Pagan Enterprises, and Ronnie Hopkins Enterprises. All three make between 150 to 200 chassis for cars on the Winston Cup, Busch Grand National, and NASCAR Craftsman Truck Series. Typically, these companies can build anything from the frame up. Teams can purchase the frame only, a completed chassis, or a completed car. Usually, however, teams buy a complete chassis consisting of the frame, an extensive roll cage, and the interior floor pan. All of these parts are made by hand to exact specifications using NASCAR's rule book and the team's input as a guide.

It takes about 600 pounds of tubular steel to build a typical chassis and takes between 45 and 70 hours to complete. Depending on what the team requests, a chassis can cost between $6,500 and $8,000.

To build a frame, the team or manufacturer starts with a jig, an object that holds all the different parts in their correct positions. Using a jig allows teams to duplicate the same design and helps make sure the frame is straight.

Using raw materials, the builders then cut, bend, and weld the parts into position. Teams can choose the height of the side frame rails and the width of the material. For example, the left side frame rail is usually one-half inch higher to allow room for the exhaust, which will be added later. They also can choose the width of the trailer arm cross member, which sits between the frame rails and holds the mounts for the rear suspension system.

The roll cage is built separately, then added when the frame is complete. The cage, a web of tubular steel bent to fit around the driver, is designed to protect him in case of a crash. In the early days of racing, cars were not equipped with roll cages. If a car flipped over during an accident, the roof usually caved in, causing injury to the driver. Early roll cages were nothing more than two-by-four boards nailed together. Eventually metal was used, and the roll cage evolved into what it is today, an integral structure of the car that saves lives.

Roll cages are made from seamless tubing with .095" wall thickness and are 1.75" wide. The main structure of the cage is the same on all cars, although there is some variation in style depending on the make. Once the cage is completed, it is welded to the frame. The next stage of construction includes the addition of bars extending from the roll cage to the front and rear portions of the car. A sheet metal floor pan and firewall are added to the vehicle. The chassis is then shipped to the team's shop, where it is well on its way to becoming a race car.

4

THE NEXT STEP

Once a team has built or acquired a chassis, the car building goes into high gear.

It takes about 80 man-days to get a car ready for the road, which means eight crew members working for 10 days straight to complete the car, although it often takes two weeks or more. It can be, and has been, done much faster when a driver has wrecked a car needed for the next race. Ideally, however, teams prefer not to have to put together such a complex project in such a short time.

Before crew members add any new parts to the chassis, they take time to go over the frame, carefully measuring and positioning all the mounting brackets and the overall alignment of the chassis. Once the team has confirmed that the chassis meets their re-

Front view of a chassis showing the oversize radiator, shock absorbers, engine block, shifter, lead weight ballast bars which are installed on both sides, seat, and seatbelts, along with the roll cage, and side steel tubing protection for the driver.

quirements, two men go to work installing various mounting brackets, such as those which hold the throttle cable, steering components, shock mounts, and the fuel cell. If the car isn't needed immediately, these men take about four days to complete the task.

After the first step is complete, the team moves the car (it is mounted on rollers throughout the process, allowing a few men to push it through the various stages of building) to the body shop where fabricators build the body.

Despite resemblance to a showroom stock model, a majority of the body panels are created by hand. The roof, the rear deck lid, and the hood of the car are the only parts that are the same as the stock model. The front grill and rear bumper are made of a composite material and are models approved by NASCAR. Everything else on the exterior of the car is built by skilled craftsmen who take raw 23-gauge (about 25 thousandths of an inch) sheet metal and bend, beat, and cut it into a smooth body. The sides of the car make up the largest span of sheet metal, which runs the full length of the vehicle. It is first cut to length, then given a slight bend using a roller, and finally held in place with small clips until welded into place. Fabricators mount and remove the parts several times before welding them into a solid shape. Every piece must fit smoothly with the one next to it and meet NASCAR specifications. In fact, before a piece is welded, the fabricators check to see if the body fits NASCAR's templates for that section of the car.

It usually takes two men a week to ten days to complete the body. They take a bit longer to

create the body of a car that is to be used on a superspeedway such as Daytona or Talladega, where a minor ding in the body will cut the car's ability to move through the air, and thereby cut down on its speed.

Aerodynamic efficiency (the ability of air to flow smoothly over the surface of the car) is not as critical on cars being driven on short tracks such as the Bristol Motor Speedway or Martinsville Speedway. As a result, fabricators

Overall top view of the Interstate Batteries-sponsored car in the pit area shows the aerodynamic clean lines needed for top speed on the race track.

do not worry as much about air efficiency when creating bodies for short-track cars.

After the exterior is done, the car is rolled to yet another part of the shop where the interior will be constructed. Over a period of five days, four crewmen will install the seat, the electrical wiring system, and the dashboard. At the same time, interior sheet metal parts are handcrafted and installed. All windows—purchased from an outside company—are then trimmed and installed.

After the crewmen have spent more than a week building the car, they take out all of the interior parts and windows, leaving only the body and the interior sheet metal. This is done so that other members of the crew working in the paint shop—another area of the shop—can paint the interior and exterior of the car without worrying about painting over important parts.

The inside of the car is painted first. Most teams use either grey, white, or red paint for the interior. Then the outside of the car is spayed various colors, depending on the paint scheme. After the paint is dry, sponsor decals, numbers, and the various stickers required to race under NASCAR's rules are added.

When the paint has cured, four men spend five days putting the car back together again. This time, they add the radiator, the brake system, the engine, transmission, and all of the other necessary parts.

Finally, two men spend about a day making final adjustments to the car. This includes setting up the car with the appropriate weight balance, which could mean adding up to 250 pounds of lead to the car's chassis or making sure it is not heavier than NASCAR's required 3,400-pound minimum weight. Every pound over the minimum weight slows the car.

After every part has been checked over and over again, the car is finally ready to be tested at the race track. All totaled, the car will have cost about $125,000.

5

HEARTBEAT OF THE CAR

If the chassis of a race car is compared to the human skeleton, a race car's engine is the equivalent of the heart.

When fed 108 octane race fuel (the typical street car uses 87 octane gas) the engine comes to life, sending nearly 750 hp flowing through the drive train and the rear wheels.

Winston Cup cars use 358 c.i., eight-cylinder engines based on a design introduced in the 1950s. During the past three decades, crew members have worked hard to squeeze every ounce of horsepower out of the engines in order to make the cars go faster.

As with the chassis, teams either build their own motors or buy them from an outside supplier. The decision to build or buy motors is based on many of the same factors that go into building or buying chassis. It takes many people, floor space, and a great deal of technological know-how to turn out the engines used

Crew members of a NASCAR team work on a Chevrolet V-8 engine before installing it in one of their team's race cars.

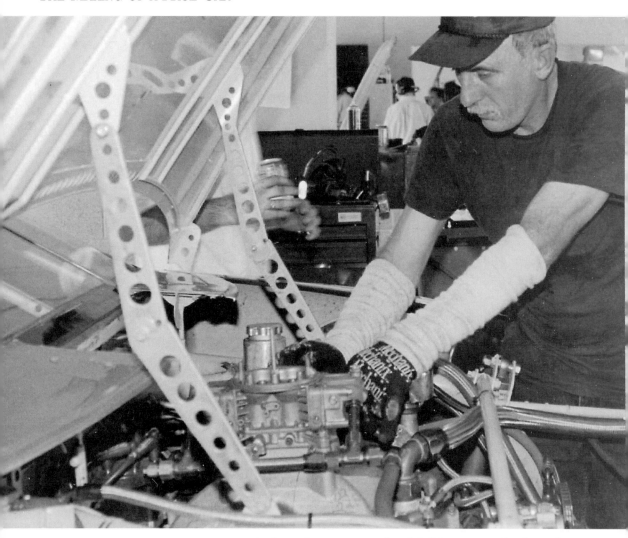

Ed Penland checks over driver Randy Porter's Ford engine before practice runs at the Jiffy Lube 300 at Homestead Motorsports Complex in Homestead, Florida.

today. A team can build 20 motors before they find the one that meets their needs for a given race. Doing so costs money: lots of it. A Winston Cup motor costs about $40,000. Teams can lease them from engine suppliers for between $25,000 and $30,000, but they have to return the parts when finished with them. Either way, it's a pretty steep investment for a part that can explode at any moment during a race, remove the driver from contention, and ruin hours and days of engineering time.

During NASCAR's five decades in existence, the engine has been a major focus of attention. During one stretch in the 1960s, auto manufacturers went through a bigger-is-better phase. As they realized that being first on the track helped push sales at their dealerships, the automakers started to build bigger, heavier cars that contained larger, faster engines.

Whereas today's cars use 358 c.i. motors, in the 1960s, car makers fitted race cars with 455 c.i. beasts. When the situation got out of hand, NASCAR stepped in and required cars to use motors that did not exceed 358 c.i.

The Chevrolet V-8 engine—as it is known today—was developed by the manufacturer in 1955. At the time, the company's chief engineer, Ed Cole, persuaded company management that there was a need for an entry level, high performance engine. With the help of engineer Zora Arkus-Duntov, Cole pushed the concept of a racing motor that until 1998 was the standard for racing. Ironically, Chevrolet managers frowned on racing in the late 1950s, forcing Arkus-Duntov to rely on others to get the racing secrets to the race teams at the track. Today, using what they have learned over time through hard work and countless hours of testing, engine builders are creating the strongest cars in the history of stock car racing. But even with all that, companies continue to seek better ways to build engines.

For the 1998 season, Chevrolet introduced the SB2 engine, which according to Doug Duchardt, General Motors Motorsports Engine manager, marks the greatest change in racing engines since the Chevrolet V-8 debuted in 1955. "It's been going on for three years," Duchardt said of the development process. "We started it in 1994 and presented it to NASCAR in October 1995. We revised the cylinder head and presented it to NASCAR in May 1997. The revised SB2 is what we're running [in 1998]."

The Chevrolet engine was developed using direct input from a handful of NASCAR teams. In the past, auto manufacturers would build a new engine and take it to the race teams for

Two crew members work on a Ford V-8 engine in the new Taurus, first utilized in the NASCAR 1998 racing season.

their input. This time around, however, the teams helped create the new design. "It gained instant credibility," Duchardt said of the motor. "[The teams] knew the guys who developed them were racing every weekend. It wasn't us doing it in a vacuum."

The main engine block for Fords and Chevrolets (which are also used in Pontiacs) are made by the manufacturer. The blocks, or main portion, of the engine are modified specifically for racing, with many of the parts used in street cars removed. For example, race cars use external oil filters and oil tanks, making the oil filter mount built onto the block obsolete. So the manufacturer removed the mount. And the cooling system holes are now widened to provide optimum cooling efficiency in race conditions.

Once the block arrives at the engine building shop, the crew goes to work preparing it for the next step. They adjust the size of the cylinders, the seats for the cam, and the height of the deck where the cylinder heads sit. They go over each part carefully before installing anything on the motor. A little extra time here saves headaches down the road.

The first part installed on the motor is the crankshaft. The pistons, connecting rods, wrist pins, and rings are added next. Then the cam shaft is added with all its necessary hardware and mounting parts.

At this point, the engine is ready for the cylinder heads, which have been prepared separately. Next is the intake manifold, which has been altered by the engine builders to their own specifications, although still within NASCAR's guidelines. The manifold controls the way air and fuel are mixed before reaching

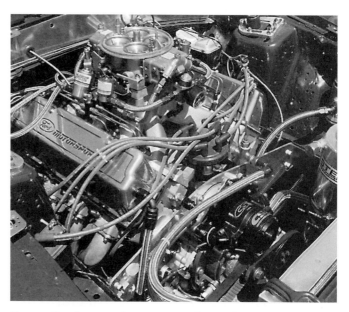

Doug Mangrum's 1988 Ford V-8 Mustang GT engine is similar to the Ford V-8 engines used in NASCAR racing. Mangrum set a national record of over 174 mph for the quarter-mile at the Mobil 1 World Ford Challenge in Bowling Green, Kentucky, May 15–17, 1998.

the cylinder and is critical to the overall performance of the car.

Finally the valve covers, oil pump, belts, a fan, the alternator, and the appropriate wiring are added.

When the motor is complete, the engine builders mount it on a dynamometer, a machine which tests the horsepower and durability of the motor (it is called the "dyno"). By using this machine, engine builders can adjust the fuel-to-air ratios to create peak horsepower. When they are finished with the dyno, the engine is ready to be installed in the car and tested on the track.

All totaled, 120 man-hours are spent building a single engine. And at any given time, the typical race team has 20 engines available for use. Some of those are for general use, whereas others, called restrictor-plate engines, are used on the superspeedways such as Daytona and Talladega.

In 1988, NASCAR introduced restrictor plates, small metal plates that sit between the carburetor and the intake manifold, which act to reduce horsepower to cut the speeds of the cars at the faster tracks. At the time, speeds were in excess of 200 mph and were reaching dangerous levels, not only for the drivers but also for the fans. NASCAR feared a car going 200 mph might become airborne in a crash, sending it into the bleachers. In an effort to avoid such a calamity, the sanctioning body ruled the plates had to be installed.

The addition of restrictor plates caused engine builders much grief because it took them one solid month to prepare engines specifically for the February running of the Daytona 500.

Engine builders have often been compared to scientists who tinker with several ideas before finally finding the long unknown answer to a question. For engine builders, those answers come in horsepower equivalents. For every seven horsepower that can be found, a car will go one mph faster on the track. "Everybody works so hard," said Bobby Hamilton, driver of the Kodak Chevrolet. "It's mindboggling to see what they can do. . . . They just have to get in there and dig and learn those new combinations. There will be a time when all the rule changes run out and they'll have to go back to something. [But], no matter how much power you've got, the engine has to last. Durability means a lot."

THE SPONSORS

Besides the gut-rumbling roar of the engines, the first thing you notice about a stock car is its color and paint scheme.

Today's racers combine elaborate paint patterns with sponsor decals to create advertising billboards that travel at speeds at or above 200 mph. In fact, most people remember a car and its driver by the name of the sponsor painted on the side.

Sponsors are a key factor in racing. Although costs vary, the top-ranked teams receive as much as $6 million a year to allow a corporation to put its name on the side and hood of their vehicles. The primary sponsor, the one who pays the most and gets the largest percentage of available space on the car, is the one that calls the shots when deciding the color and overall look of the race car. That's because the sponsors use the cars to promote their

Dale Jarrett's Kellogg's-sponsored car on the track. The design features bright red and white lettering against a brilliant yellow background. The large numbers on the top are yellow against a deep red background.

products. For example, McDonald's hopes that having its name on the side of a race car will generate higher sales at their fast-food restaurants. By paying a team owner to be the primary sponsor, the company makes the car part of their general marketing plan.

Although the company funneling the largest amount of money to the team has a major say in the way the car looks, it does not mean that the sponsor can select colors and patterns at random. Just the opposite is true. A great deal of research and discussion goes into deciding how the car will look on the track.

Usually companies go to an outside design firm to develop an eye-pleasing pattern. Before

Sponsor decals on Dale Jarrett's right front fender.

they make a final decision, the designers, the company, and the team meet to determine if the planned look can be easily duplicated at the team's shop. What they are looking for is a design appealing to both fans at the track and those watching at home. They also want the fans to remember the name on the side of the car.

Most cars on the track use one basic color with the sponsor's logo added as a decal later. Some designs, however, are more elaborate, multi-colored schemes and require several steps in the paint shop before the final decals are applied.

The left rear fender of Dale Jarrett's car shows additional sponsorship decals.

For a sport that is more than 50 years old, brightly colored cars and elaborate sponsor decals are something relatively new. In the early days, the only thing on the sides of the cars were their numbers, and those were made of tape so they could be removed for the drive home. By the late 1950s, however, most drivers were using their cars just for racing, and the days of driving a car to the track, racing it, then driving back home were almost over. As a result, drivers turned to sign painters to apply numbers to the roof and sides of their cars. At that time, NASCAR required only that the engine's factory-set horsepower number appear on the hood of the car.

In the 1960s, the concept of sponsorship started to emerge and brought along with it the idea of putting decals and logos on the cars. The initial attempts to put sponsors' names on cars were done with crudely de-

Bobby Labonte's Interstate Batteries car rooftop numbers.

signed logos that were printed on paper and then taped to the cars.

Then along came vinyl decals and numbers.

By the mid 1960s, NASCAR required all cars to display the engine's cubic-inch measurement on the hood (in place of the horsepower numbers), 18-inch-high car numbers on the door and rear deck lid, and a 36-inch-high number on the roof. The rooftop number had to be read from the driver's side so that scorers sitting in the infield could keep track of the cars. And NASCAR limited the sponsor's name to letters no larger than six inches high.

Today the rules are similar. Of course, sponsor names have become larger and the minimum size for rooftop numbers is now 32 inches high.

NASCAR prohibits the use of slogans on the car. Teams can load up the cars with as many sponsor logos as they want, but they cannot print any catchy slogans. And NASCAR requires that smaller decals be carried on the cars as part of the corporation's sponsorship deals. The smaller stickers, however, are part of contingency sponsorship programs that provide drivers with specific performance bonuses.

TESTING

Building a car is only half the work of readying a car for NASCAR's premiere level of stock car racing. Before the green flag starts the first race of the season, teams will spend several days testing at the Daytona International Speedway and elsewhere to prepare for the coming season.

Testing is important for several reasons. Going to the track ahead of time gives crews a chance to check over new parts, engines, and the overall handling of the car well before race day. It is also important for the driver, who may not be familiar with a particular body style, engine, or the performance changes that occurred during the off season. And testing helps teams get the cars as close to race-ready as possible before they actually return to the track for the race. By doing preliminary work before race weekend, teams can find problems before they happen.

Dale Jarrett's Ford Taurus in the garage after running test laps. Mechanics adjust springs, shocks, and the swaybar to modify the way a car handles in turns and how it impacts the track.

With each new rule and each new area of technology limited by NASCAR, teams are forced to work harder to go faster. Getting a car to run at peak performance is a delicate balance between horsepower, aerodynamics, and handling.

In the 1990s, aerodynamics has been one of the most important and most tested areas. Simply put, the more easily the car moves through the wind, the faster it will go. Teams are always looking for ways to cut a car's wind resistance, or drag, and to find a combination of low drag with high downforce (air pressure that holds the car onto the track in the turns).

Initial efforts to improve aerodynamics begin at the team's body shop, where all lines, grooves, and bangs in the car body are filled with body putty to create a smooth surface over which the wind can flow. Even the smallest nick on the surface of the car could cause the car to slow down.

After the work in the shop is completed, testing is held on the race track and in a wind tunnel.

A wind tunnel is a huge room with fans that create winds up to 200 mph. The car is hooked up to a computer system that follows the vehicle's motion. The wind simulates race track action and allows the teams to see how the car will react at top speed. By using smoke, engineers are able to see how the wind flows up, over, and around the car. Usually teams take several body parts to the test to see which design works best within NASCAR's rules.

The goal throughout is to lower the car's overall drag count, or resistance to the wind. Drag is measured in counts. In the wind tunnel, seven counts equal one mph on the track.

But the wind tunnel cannot answer all the questions engineers have about a car. For example, although the tunnel can recreate certain on-track characteristics, it cannot take into account how the car flexes during a race or compensates for the way the tires move in and out of the fender during a race, which results in increased wind resistance. "The difference in the wind tunnel is that we can simulate the ride height to a point, but there is no moving ground plane for the wind tunnel," said Preston Miller, technical manager for Ford's Winston Cup program. "It's a full-sized tunnel and the floor air is not the same as the car moving over the ground. . . . The only way to find out how fast a car will go on any track is to actually go to that track and run the car."

Jeff Gordon runs test laps to check how the car feels on the track, after which he will confer with his crew team members to make adjustments.

Using a wind tunnel is not cheap. A typical eight-hour stay costs more than $20,000 and makes every minute inside important. What the wind tunnel does, however, is give teams a general idea of how much work is ahead of them. Most teams look for a baseline of their tunnel tests, which they use as a starting point for further testing.

Under NASCAR rules, each team gets seven three-day test sessions during the season to use at any track staging a Winston Cup event. Most teams use at least two of those tests at Daytona or Talladega before the season starts. They save the rest for key races during the season.

Testing also gives teams a chance to use on-board computers that are otherwise banned from the sport. Before going onto the track, sensors are placed at key points throughout the car to collect data about the car's performance. With that data, teams can make adjustments to the car to gain more speed. NASCAR prohibits the use of such computers during a race, although they are legal in practice.

A typical test session consists of drivers making several laps and then returning to the garage, where they consult with team members. After more changes, they go back out to see if they are making progress.

Besides adjusting cars to the new rules, testing allows the teams a chance to find out how their car will handle when running on the track with other vehicles. When one car runs behind another, the performance of both is affected as they cut through the air. This effect, called "drafting," cannot be tested in a wind tunnel.

In practice, provided the car is running reasonably well, teams work on handling and on improving the driver's comfort level on the track. They do this by changing springs to affect the way the car handles through the turns or by adjusting shocks, which impact the way the car reacts to the track. Getting a car just right, however, is left up to a chassis specialist, who can also adjust the sway bar to control the way the car's weight shifts in turns and make changes in the other steering components.

Crew members rely on the drivers to tell them how the car is handling, such as whether it is "neutral," "loose," or "pushing." A neutral car is what they strive for, although it is difficult to accomplish. If the car is loose, it feels like the back end is going to break loose from the track and spin. If the car is pushing, it feels like it is going to go straight to the wall.

Chassis specialist of the Interstate Batteries-sponsored car makes fine tune adjustments to the front suspension and braking systems.

The first step in finding the right balance is usually accomplished by adjusting the wedge, which changes the amount of the car's total weight allotted to each wheel. For example, adding more weight to the left rear wheel—done by slipping a socket wrench through a hole in the rear window—takes weight off the right front wheel.

While testing ultimately benefits the drivers, it is also a tedious process. "I'm bored to death out there [testing]," said two-time champion Jeff Gordon after a Daytona test. "What we're doing right now is for the engineers and the crew members and for [crew chief] Ray [Evernham]. They built these cars and went to the wind tunnel and they've got these things on their lists to try. All I am is just another computer chip that's plugged into the seat to push the pedal down."

Everything is done for research and development, Gordon said. "That's what a test is all about," he added. "You try different manifolds, carburetors, it's really fine tuning now. We won't see any big gains, and hopefully we won't see any big losses either."

As NASCAR has moved to eliminate any grey areas in the rule book, it has also clamped down on areas in which teams can experiment to gain more speed. These days, no team expects to make a giant leap in performance during a test. "I don't care how many things you're testing, you're just looking for small gains," said seven-time champion Dale Earnhardt. "If you've made some gains, you feel good about what you've accomplished."

According to Earnhardt, if NASCAR makes a rule change, teams have to work harder to get back what they lost in performance because of the new rule. "When NASCAR changes the mark, whether it be a restrictor plate change or with the bodies, when they come up with the rules, it pushes the market on technology," he said. "Then you put more time into trying to get around it and trying to get the advantage back you lost. They keep pushing the mark, and we keep pushing the mark."

SAFETY

Ask any Winston Cup driver about the safety of his car, and he will tell you he feels safer in his race car than he does driving on the highway with everyday drivers.

That's easy to say, of course, because when the drivers are in their cars, they are strapped into specially built seats and surrounded by a web of steel tubing that helps stop the cars from caving in during a crash. But that isn't the only safety feature built into today's racers. There is webbing across the driver's side window to protect them from flying debris and to help keep them in the car. There are five-point seat belts that hold them tightly in their seats, and the cars are equipped with rubber bladders to hold the fuel to help prevent fires. So it is easy to see why the drivers feel safe while going so fast.

Today's safety features, considered standard and necessary, evolved over time. Car design-

Rusty Wallace awaits instructions from his crew. Safety features such as window netting, hard steel tubing, and fuel cells are now standard.

ers, drivers, and team owners used past wrecks as research projects to come up with new devices to help protect the drivers' lives. To say the safety aspect has come a long way from the early days of NASCAR would be an understatement.

When the sport started, there was virtually no concern for safety. It is not that the people involved didn't care about the drivers; it just wasn't a consideration until disaster struck. Moreover, because the cars were supposed to be stock, there was little room in the rules for add-on parts.

Look at some photographs from the first decade of NASCAR racing. The men were usually wearing short-sleeved shirts, regular pants, and whatever makeshift helmets they could find. There was no such thing as fireproof driving suits or high-impact helmets. "I raced with whatever I had on, whatever it was I was wearing when I got to the track," said Herb Thomas, the 1951 and 1953 series champion. "We never even thought about flame-retardant material. The helmets we used weren't much, either," he continued. "I don't remember what the shell was made of but it was just enough to cover the top of my head. There wasn't much insulation inside, no real padding like they have now. The inside was leather that came down to the leather straps that covered my ears. That was it."

It is easy to see how dangerous the sport was back then and how daring the drivers were.

In the 1940s and 1950s, seatbelts were not standard equipment in street cars. As a result, they were not part of the racing scene either. And there was no such a thing as a roll cage. Today's roll cages are mechanical marvels that create a cocoon around the drivers.

NASCAR's first official rule-book mention of roll bars was in 1953 when the sanctioning body recommended a metal hoop to go up and behind the driver's head. The device was required by NASCAR in 1955, and additional interior roll bars were soon added.

By 1960, NASCAR required cars to have a full, four-point roll cage with a single brace behind the driver. Soon after, they created bars along the door sides to protect the drivers in side-impact crashes. In 1965, two bars were required on the side of the cage, and two years later, four bars on the sides were required. Under NASCAR's rules, teams could add more

Dale Jarrett in his race car, with his safety helmet in his hand, confers with his pit crew. The side impact head protection as well as the steel tube roll cage have been developed to protect the driver in case of a rollover.

bars as long as officials could determine the teams were not adding the extra steel to gain a competitive advantage. Today, NASCAR rules stipulate where bars must be placed and the thickness of the tubing used to create the cage.

After a few serious fires in the mid 1960s, including the 1964 crash and fire that led to the death of Glenn "Fireball" Roberts, engineers created the fuel cell, a rubber bladder that prevents gas from sloshing around and spilling in a crash. Those early fires also led to the creation of the firesuit, which is made of a fire-resistant material that helps protect drivers.

Seatbelts, which started out as pieces of rope, evolved into high-strength straps which hold the driver snug in his or her seat.

"Things happen so fast in this industry that what we produce now is light years ahead of where we were ten years ago," said Bill Simpson, chief executive officer of Team Simpson Racing, a leading motorsports safety apparel and equipment company. "As a former driver, I know first-hand how important it is for a driver to be able to rely on his safety equipment. We work closely with the drivers and teams to provide them with the ultimate in safety equipment."

Ironically, because of the work done by Simpson and others, drivers of today probably worry about safety as little as Herb Thomas did in the 1950s, although for many different reasons.

GLOSSARY

A-arm	A component of the front suspension system on all stock cars.
Apron	The flat paved portion of the race track closest to the infield.
Banking	The slope of the racing surface measured in degrees.
Bite	A reference to the way a car is gripping the track.
Blister	A swelling on a tire's surface that forms when the tire gets too hot.
Camber	A reference to the angle of a car's wheels in relation to the chassis.
Carburetor	A device mounted to the top of the intake manifold, which regulates fuel fed to the engine.
Chassis	The foundation of a race car, which includes the roll cage, interior sheet metal, and other parts.
Coefficient of Drag	A mathematical term to measure aerodynamic efficiency.
Downforce	The aerodynamic pressure on a car measured in pounds.
Drafting	Two cars running nose to tail to minimize their combined wind resistance.
Groove	The preferred line around a race track.
Loose	A handling condition in which the rear tires lose grip with the race track.
Marbles	Small pieces of rubber, dirt, and other matter that collect near the top of the race track.
Pit Road	An area just off the race track where teams perform in-race servicing of their cars. Also known as pit row and pit lane.
Restrictor Plate	A small metal plate with four holes that is inserted between the carburetor and the intake manifold to reduce airflow and horsepower.
Scuffs	Tires that have been used during a practice session in preparation for a race.
Set-up	Adjustments made to a car to create an optimum driving condition.
Short Track	A track less than a mile in length.
Speedway	A track longer than a mile though not more than 1.5 miles.
Spoiler	A piece of metal extending across the rear end of the car that helps create downforce on the rear wheels.
Stickers	Brand new tires that still have the manufacturer's information stickers on them.
Superspeedway	An oval track more than 1.5 miles long.
Tight	Handling condition in which the car's front tires lose grip with the track before the rear.

FURTHER READING

Center, Bill. *NASCAR: The Thunder of America.* New York: Harper Collins, 1998.

Chapin, Kim. *Fast As White Lightning.* New York: The Dial Press, 1981.

Golenbock, Peter, and Greg Fielden. *The Stock Car Racing Encyclopedia.* Indianapolis: Macmillan, 1997.

Huff, Richard. *Behind the Wall: A Season on the NASCAR Circuit.* Chicago: Bonus Books, 1992.

Huff, Richard. *The Insider's Guide to Stock Car Racing.* Chicago: Bonus Books, 1997.

Pearce, Al, and Bill Fleischman. *Inside Sports Magazine NASCAR Racing: The Ultimate Fan Guide.* Detroit: Visible Ink, 1998.

ACKNOWLEDGMENTS

The author would like to thank the following people, without whose help the creation of this book would have been impossible: Michelle and Ryan Huff, Mom, and Cathe Slocum.

ABOUT THE AUTHOR

Richard Huff is an award-winning journalist and author. His previous books include *Behind the Wall: A Season on the NASCAR Circuit*; *The Insider's Guide to Stock Car Racing*; and *Formula One Racing*. He is a staff writer and motor sports columnist for the New York *Daily News*. His work has appeared in such national publications as *NASCAR Magazine*, *Inside NASCAR*, *Stock Car Racing Magazine*, *Video Review*, *The Washington Journalism Review*, *Seventeen*, and *Hot Rod, Jr.* He lives in Highland, New Jersey, with his wife, Michelle, and son, Ryan.

INDEX